SURVIVING THE STORM:

Navigating conflict and cultivating resilience for a thriving future

By

Gary D. Gates

Copyright

Copyright © Gary D. Gates 2024. All rights reserved. This document and its contents are protected under international copyright laws. No part of this document may be reproduced, distributed, or transmitted in any form or by any means, including photocopying, recording, or other electronic or mechanical methods, without the prior written permission of the copyright holder, except in the case of brief quotations embodied in critical reviews and certain other noncommercial uses permitted by copyright law.

Table of content

Copyright
Table of content
Introduction
The Power of Resilience: Growth in the Face of Adversity.
From Surviving to Thriving: Thriving in the Face of Adversity.
Navigating Change: Adapting to Shifting Environments
Building Bridges: Fostering Positive Relationships in Conflict.
   chapter 1
Recognizing Different Types of Conflict.
Interpersonal Conflict
Intrapersonal Conflict
Organizational Conflict

Intergroup Conflict
Environmental Conflict
Cultural Conflict

Chapter 2
Exploring the Psychology of Conflict
i. Cognitive Biases and Perception
ii. Emotional Dynamics and Reactivity
iii. Social Identity and Group Dynamics

Chapter 3
Navigating the Storm: Strategies for Managing Conflict
i. Understanding the Nature of Conflict
ii. Cultivating Self-Awareness and Emotional Regulation
iii. Developing Effective Communication Skills

iv Fostering Empathy and Perspective-Taking
v. Collaborative Problem-Solving and Negotiation
vi. Setting Boundaries and Asserting Rights
vii. Seeking Support and Collaboration

Chapter 4
Communication Techniques for Conflict
i. Active Listening
ii. Assertive Communication
iii. Nonviolent Communication (NVC)
iv. Reflective Listening
v. Emotional Regulation and Self-Control

Chapter 5
Anchoring Your Ship: Building Resilience in Times of Crisis
i. Understanding Resilience
ii. Cultivating Emotional Resilience
iii. Strengthening Cognitive Resilience
iv. Building social resilience
v. Learning from Adversity
vi. Practical techniques for cultivating resilience

Chapter 6
Finding Opportunity in Challenge
i. Embracing a Growth Mindset
ii. Cultivating Resilience
iii. Finding Meaning and Purpose
iv. Fostering adaptability and flexibility

v. Accepting Failure as a Stepping Stone to Success
vi. Cultivating Gratitude and Optimism
vii. Seeking Opportunities for Growth and Learning

Chapter 7
Cultivating a Growth Mindset: Embracing the Power of Growth and Learning
i. Understanding the Growth Mindset
ii. Embracing Challenges as Opportunities for Growth
iii. Viewing Failure as a Stepping Stone to Success

Chapter 8
Conflict Transformation: Moving Beyond Resolution

i. Understanding Conflict Transformation
ii. Moving Beyond Win-Lose Dynamics
iii. Fostering Empathy and Understanding
iv. Addressing structural injustice and inequality
v. Promoting Healing and Reconciliation
vi. Empowering Individuals and Communities

Chapter 9
Turning Setbacks into Stepping Stones: Harnessing Adversity for Growth and Success.
i. Understanding Setbacks
ii. Accepting failure as a prelude to achievement

iii. Cultivating Resilience in the Face of Adversity.
iv. Finding Meaning and Purpose in Adversity
v. Turning Obstacles into Opportunities
vi. Cultivating a Growth Mindset
vii. Seeking support and guidance
Conclusion
Sailing into the Future: Charting Your Course of Thrive
Reflecting on Lessons Learned
Creating Your Personal Resilience Plan.

Introduction

Conflict frequently manifests itself as a storm on the turbulent waters of life, posing a threat to derail our ships and leaving us adrift in a sea of uncertainty. There is, nevertheless, a potential for development, resiliency, and ultimately, a prosperous future that resides within the core of conflict. We are pleased to welcome you to the book "Surviving the Storm: Navigating Conflict and Cultivating Resilience for a Thriving Future," in which we will embark on a journey to gain an understanding of the nature of conflict, discover strategies for navigating the turbulent waters of conflict, and harness the power of resilience to emerge stronger and more resilient than we have ever been before.

unveiling the storm

In the first part of our journey, we set sail into the heart of the conflict to decipher its complexity and gain an understanding of the dynamics that lie behind it. We investigate the various manifestations that conflict can take, ranging from disagreements between individuals to bigger tensions in society, and we conduct an in-depth investigation into the psychological factors that underlie our reactions to conflict. By shining light on the nature of conflict, we lay the groundwork for handling the issues that conflict presents with clarity and insight.

The Power of Resilience: Growth in the Face of Adversity

As we continue to go deeper into the core of the dispute, we come to realize the transforming power of resilience, which allows us to turn challenges into opportunities. In this chapter, we study how resilience enables us to discover progress amidst difficulty, creating resilience in both our personal and professional lives. Through real-life stories of triumph over hardship, we get inspiration and insight into the unlimited ability of the human spirit to thrive in the face of adversity

From Surviving to Thriving: Thriving in the Face of Adversity. Beyond simply survival is the possibility of thriving and flourishing in the face of difficulty and adversity. In this chapter, we delve into the mental modifications and behavioral strategies essential to transforming from merely surviving to thriving. By embracing a growth mindset and reframing setbacks as chances for progress, we unlock the door to a future filled with possibility and potential.

Navigating Change: Adapting to Shifting Environments

As the winds of change sweep across the oceans of life, we are called upon to adapt and evolve in response. In this chapter, we explore the art of navigating change, studying ways to embrace ambiguity, and adapting to shifting surroundings with grace and resilience. By utilizing the power of flexibility and resilience, we traverse the ever-changing currents of life with confidence and ease. relationships

Building Bridges: Fostering Positive Relationships in Conflict. At the core of conflict lies the opportunity to construct bridges of understanding and connection, forging stronger and more resilient bonds in the process. In this chapter, we explore the transformative potential of conflict transformation, moving beyond mere resolution to build permanent peace and harmony. Through the growth of empathy, compassion, and constructive communication, we prepare the road for deeper, more meaningful relationships founded on a foundation of trust and understanding.

Chapter 1

Recognizing Different Types of Conflict.

Conflict is a multidimensional phenomenon that unfolds in numerous forms, each bringing its unique problems and prospects for settlement. To effectively navigate the stormy seas of conflict, it is vital to have an understanding of the numerous types of conflict that may happen in our personal and professional lives. By understanding these many forms of conflict, we may better equip ourselves with the tools and tactics necessary to face them with clarity, compassion, and resilience.

Interpersonal Conflict

One of the most common forms of conflict is interpersonal conflict, which happens between people or small groups within a wider societal environment. Interpersonal conflict can happen in a variety of circumstances, from arguments between friends or family members to confrontations between coworkers or romantic partners. These confrontations may be sparked by differences in values, views, personalities, or communication styles and can escalate quickly if not addressed swiftly and effectively.

Intrapersonal Conflict

In addition to disputes between persons, conflict can also emerge within the individual themselves in the form of intrapersonal conflict. Intrapersonal conflict arises when an individual has opposing thoughts, feelings, or desires within themselves, leading to inner turmoil and misery. This form of conflict may come from competing goals or priorities, unresolved previous traumas, or cognitive dissonance between one's views and actions. Intrapersonal conflict can be particularly tough to handle, as it needs introspection, self-awareness, and emotional regulation to resolve efficiently.

Organizational Conflict

Conflict can also arise within organizations when individuals or groups have differing interests, goals, or priorities that come into conflict with one another. Organizational conflict can originate from a variety of factors, including rivalry for resources, power battles between executives or departments, or disagreements about strategic direction or decision-making processes. Left uncontrolled, organizational conflict can lead to diminished morale, productivity, and innovation, as well as increased turnover and dysfunction inside the organization.

Intergroup Conflict

Beyond conflicts between individuals or inside organizations, conflict can also arise between distinct groups within society, a phenomenon known as intergroup conflict. Intergroup conflict can emerge along lines of race, ethnicity, religion, nationality, socioeconomic status, or political affiliation and may be driven by prejudice, discrimination, inequity, or historical grievances. Intergroup conflict can have far-reaching implications, including societal discontent, violence, and even war, making it vital to confront and resolve such disputes via communication, reconciliation, and collective action.

Environmental Conflict

Another increasingly prominent form of conflict is environmental conflict, which arises over competing interests or values related to the use and management of natural resources and ecosystems. Environmental conflicts may entail disagreements over land use, water rights, pollution, conservation, or climate change mitigation and adaptation. These conflicts often pit multiple stakeholders, such as governments, companies, local communities, and environmental activists, against one another, highlighting the intricate interplay between economic development, environmental sustainability, and social justice

Cultural Conflict

Finally, conflict can also emerge between distinct cultural groupings as individuals and society cope with diverse worldviews, practices, and traditions. Cultural conflict may appear in confrontations over language, religion, gender roles, or cultural customs and can lead to misunderstandings, stereotypes, and discrimination. In an increasingly interconnected and diverse world, cultural conflict brings both problems and opportunities for conversation, mutual tolerance, and intercultural understanding.

Chapter 2

Exploring the Psychology of Conflict

Conflict is a very human experience, founded on the intricate interplay of thoughts, emotions, perceptions, and acts. By diving into the psychology of conflict, we gain insight into the fundamental motivations of conflict escalation and resolution and identify ways for negotiating conflict with understanding, compassion, and resilience. In this inquiry, we will examine the psychological mechanisms that determine our responses to conflict, from the cognitive biases that influence our perceptions to the emotional dynamics that fuel our emotions.

i.Cognitive Biases and Perception

At the heart of the psychology of conflict lies the function of cognitive biases in affecting our perceptions of ourselves, others, and the world around us. Though they help our brains swiftly and effectively absorb information, cognitive biases can also lead to mistakes in judgment and decision-making, especially in the setting of conflict. One prevalent cognitive bias is the fundamental attribution mistake, which leads us to attribute others' conduct to their character or personality traits rather than situational considerations. This inclination can fuel conflict by generating misunderstandings, stereotypes, and interpersonal conflicts.

Another cognitive bias that affects our perceptions of conflict is confirmation bias, which drives us to seek out information that confirms our preexisting views or attitudes while disregarding or discounting evidence that contradicts them. In the context of conflict, confirmation bias can strengthen existing divides and inhibit productive communication and problem-solving attempts. By becoming aware of these cognitive biases and their impact on our perceptions, we may make efforts to limit their influence and approach conflict with better objectivity and open-mindedness.

ii. Emotional Dynamics and Reactivity

In addition to cognitive biases, the psychology of conflict is also impacted by the emotional dynamics that drive our reactions to conflict situations. Conflict frequently provokes a range of deep feelings, including anger, fear, frustration, and grief, which can distort our judgment and fuel reactive, defensive responses. These emotional responses are based on our evolutionary history when they worked to shield us from imagined threats and dangers. However, in the modern environment, these same emotional responses can aggravate conflict and inhibit productive resolution efforts.

One fundamental idea in the psychology of conflict is emotional intelligence, which refers to the ability to detect, comprehend, and manage our own emotions as well as the emotions of others. By growing emotional intelligence, we can cultivate better self-awareness, empathy, and self-regulation, helping us to negotiate conflict with greater composure and efficacy. Additionally, by building a culture of emotional safety and trust, we can create an environment where individuals feel empowered to express their emotions honestly and constructively, encouraging greater understanding and connection in the face of conflict.

iii.Social Identity and Group Dynamics

Another key part of the psychology of conflict is the impact of social identity and group dynamics on determining our attitudes and behaviors toward others. Social identity theory claims that individuals get a sense of self-esteem and belonging from their membership in social groups, such as family, race, nationality, religion, or political affiliation. This sense of group identity can lead to in-group bias when individuals perceive members of their group more positively and are more likely to support and cooperate with them while perceiving members of other groups more poorly and participating in intergroup competition or conflict.

Group dynamics also play a crucial role in influencing our responses to conflict, as individuals inside groups may succumb to group norms and demands, engage in groupthink, or suffer intergroup polarization, where group members grow increasingly extreme in their attitudes and behaviors over time. These interactions can contribute to the escalation of conflict and the perpetuation of preconceptions, prejudice, and discrimination. By cultivating intergroup empathy and cooperation, we can transcend the barriers of group identity and strive towards collaborative, inclusive solutions to conflict.

Chapter 3

Navigating the Storm: Strategies for Managing Conflict

Conflict is an inevitable element of the human experience, emerging in various forms and settings throughout our lives. Whether in our relationships, professional efforts, or social interactions, conflict can bring substantial obstacles and chances for growth. In the face of conflict, we are often forced into the heart of a storm when turbulent emotions, competing interests, and divergent perspectives collide. Yet, within the center of conflict lies the opportunity for transformation, resilience, and eventually, better understanding and connection.

In this investigation of navigating the storm of conflict, we will look into successful ways of managing conflict with clarity, compassion, and resilience. Drawing upon ideas from psychology, communication theory, and conflict resolution practice, we will find practical skills and approaches for handling conflict constructively and creating positive outcomes. From establishing effective communication skills to embracing the power of empathy and collaboration, we will negotiate the complexity of conflict with grace and determination.

i. Understanding the Nature of Conflict

Before we can effectively manage the storm of conflict, it is vital to have a deeper grasp of its nature and dynamics. In this chapter, we will explore the numerous forms that conflict can take, from interpersonal conflicts to greater societal problems, and study the fundamental causes and triggers of conflict. By understanding the many manifestations of conflict and its core causes, we can begin to untangle its complexities and explore avenues toward settlement.

ii. Cultivating Self-Awareness and Emotional Regulation

Central to managing the storm of conflict is the cultivation of self-awareness and emotional regulation. In this chapter, we will study the necessity of identifying our emotional triggers, biases, and reactions in conflict situations. Through activities such as mindfulness meditation, journaling, and self-reflection, we can build better self-awareness and emotional resilience, enabling us to respond to conflict with clarity and serenity.

iii. Developing Effective Communication Skills

Effective communication lies at the heart of negotiating conflict with grace and efficacy. In this chapter, we will look into ways to develop our communication abilities, including active listening, assertive expression, and nonviolent communication. By learning to articulate our wants and concerns clearly and empathetically, while also listening attentively to the viewpoints of others, we can develop a basis for productive discourse and mutual understanding in the face of conflict.

iv Fostering Empathy and Perspective-Taking

Empathy is a potent antidote to the hostility and polarization that often precede conflict. In this chapter, we will investigate the function of empathy in building connection, understanding, and healing despite conflict. Through activities like perspective-taking, empathetic listening, and compassionate communication, we can create deeper empathy for the experiences and perspectives of others, transcending our differences and finding common ground for resolution.

v. Collaborative Problem-Solving and Negotiation

In navigating the storm of conflict, teamwork, and negotiation are key instruments for finding mutually beneficial solutions. In this chapter, we will explore the principles and strategies of collaborative problem-solving and negotiation, including interest-based negotiation, brainstorming, and consensus-building. By working together with others to find common goals and explore creative solutions, we can transform conflict into an opportunity for creativity and growth.

vi. Setting Boundaries and Asserting Rights

Navigating conflict also involves the ability to create boundaries and assert our rights and needs assertively and respectfully. In this chapter, we will review tactics for setting clear boundaries, expressing our needs and preferences assertively, and advocating for ourselves and others in the face of conflict. By creating healthy boundaries and defending our rights with confidence, we may handle conflict with integrity and self-respect.

vii. Seeking Support and Collaboration

Finally, in navigating the storm of conflict, it is crucial to identify when to seek support and collaboration from others. In this chapter, we will discuss the value of developing a support network of friends, family members, mentors, and colleagues who can offer insight, perspective, and encouragement in times of difficulty. Additionally, we will study the benefits of collaboration and coalition-building in tackling bigger societal challenges, using the potential of collective action for constructive social change.

Chapter 4

Communication Techniques for Conflict

Effective communication sits at the heart of negotiating conflict with clarity, empathy, and resilience. In the heat of confrontation, emotions run high, tensions flare, and misunderstandings abound. By honing our communication skills and adopting established approaches to handling conflict, we may create a foundation for constructive discourse, mutual understanding, and collaborative problem-solving. In this investigation of communication skills for conflict, we will delve into a range of strategies and ways for expressing ourselves assertively, listening empathetically, and creating connections in conflict's stormy seas.

i. Active Listening

Active listening is a core communication ability that forms the cornerstone of effective dispute resolution. In this chapter, we will cover the principles and strategies of active listening, including paraphrasing, clarifying, and summarizing, as well as nonverbal gestures such as eye contact, nodding, and mirroring. By listening attentively to the opinions, feelings, and needs of others, we display empathy and respect, laying the framework for constructive discourse and mutual understanding.

ii. Assertive Communication

Assertive communication is vital for expressing our wants, concerns, and boundaries assertively and respectfully in the middle of conflict. In this chapter, we will look into tactics for assertive communication, including employing "I" statements, expressing feelings and desires directly, and standing firm in the face of manipulation or pressure. By asserting ourselves confidently and assertively while remaining open to criticism and opposing ideas, we build a climate of mutual respect and empowerment in contentious situations.

iii. Nonviolent Communication (NVC)

Nonviolent Communication (NVC), founded by psychologist Marshall Rosenberg, offers a powerful framework for handling conflict with empathy, truthfulness, and compassion. In this chapter, we will investigate the four components of NVC: observation, feeling, need, and request, and learn how to use these concepts in conflict situations. By focusing on identifying and expressing our underlying sentiments and needs rather than blaming or criticizing others, we can build better understanding, connection, and collaboration amidst conflict's turbulent seas.

iv. Reflective Listening

Reflective listening is a practice that involves reflecting on the thoughts, feelings, and needs of the speaker to display empathy and understanding. In this chapter, we will explore the ideas and strategies of reflective listening, including paraphrasing, summarizing, and validating the speaker's experiences. By offering a safe and supportive space for individuals to express themselves fully and truthfully, reflective listening builds greater connection and reciprocal trust in conflict situations.

v. Emotional Regulation and Self-Control

In the heat of confrontation, emotions typically run high, making it tough to speak effectively and productively. In this chapter, we will study tools for emotional regulation and self-control, including deep breathing, mindfulness meditation, and cognitive reframing. By learning to manage our own emotional emotions and responses in conflict situations, we can approach communication with better clarity, composure, and efficacy, promoting an atmosphere of mutual respect and understanding.

vi. Conflict Resolution Model

Numerous conflict resolution models and frameworks offer assistance and structure for managing conflict effectively. In this chapter, we will investigate common conflict resolution models, such as the Thomas-Kilmann Conflict Mode Instrument (TKI), the Interest-Based Relational Approach (IBR), and the Win-Win Negotiation Model. By familiarizing ourselves with these models and their underlying principles, we may choose the most effective way to manage conflict in varied circumstances and situations, leading to positive outcomes for all parties involved.

vii. Empathetic Inquiry and Curiosity

Empathetic inquiry entails asking open-ended inquiries and demonstrating genuine curiosity about the viewpoints, feelings, and needs of others in conflict situations. In this chapter, we will explore the ability of sympathetic inquiry to develop greater knowledge, connection, and empathy despite conflict. By approaching conflict with a spirit of inquiry and openness, we create room for discourse, investigation, and mutual learning, leading the way for resolution and reconciliation.

Chapter 5

Anchoring Your Ship: Building Resilience in Times of Crisis

In the face of life's storms and trials, resilience serves as our anchor, keeping us grounded amid the chaos and unpredictability. Building resilience is vital for managing the inevitable ups and downs of life with grace, strength, and determination. In this chapter, we will explore the components of resilience, investigate the variables that lead to its growth, and identify practical ways to foster resilience in times of disaster. By anchoring our ships firmly in the harbor of resilience, we may weather the storms of life with courage, optimism, and resilience.

i. Understanding Resilience

Resilience is the ability to bounce back from adversity, adapt to change, and prosper in the face of adversity. It is not about avoiding or dismissing painful events, but rather about learning from them and developing stronger as a result. In this section, we will study the components of resilience, including emotional resilience, cognitive resilience, and social resilience, and investigate how these components interact to promote our ability to withstand adversity and thrive in spite of the challenges you are confronted with.

ii. Cultivating Emotional Resilience

Emotional resilience is the ability to cope with and bounce back from tough emotions and experiences. In this section, we will discuss ways to establish emotional resilience, including practicing self-care, forming a support network, and developing good coping skills. By learning to detect and manage our emotions effectively, we can sail through the emotional storms of life with greater ease and resilience.

iii. Strengthening Cognitive Resilience

Cognitive resilience involves the ability to maintain a positive outlook, adapt to change, and problem-solve effectively in the face of adversity. In this section, we will explore ways to develop cognitive resilience, including reframing negative ideas, practicing appreciation, and fostering a growth mindset. By cultivating optimism, adaptability, and mental agility, we may approach problems with confidence and resilience, seeing failures as chances for growth and learning.

iv. Building social resilience

Social resilience refers to the support networks and relationships that give us strength, encouragement, and connection in times of adversity. In this section, we will explore the importance of establishing social resilience through meaningful connections, community involvement, and acts of kindness and compassion. By building strong social connections and a sense of belonging, we can weather the storms of life with greater resilience and grace.

v. Learning from Adversity

Adversity is a natural part of life, and it is through facing and overcoming adversity that we grow stronger and more resilient. In this section, we will study the concept of post-traumatic growth, which refers to the positive psychological changes that can emerge as a result of enduring trauma or adversity. By reframing our experiences, finding purpose in adversity, and fostering a feeling of resilience, we can emerge from difficult circumstances with greater insight, strength, and resilience.

vi. Practical techniques for cultivating resilience

Mindfulness and meditation: Practicing mindfulness and meditation can help us stay grounded, present, and resilient in the face of stress and uncertainty.

Self-care: Taking care of our physical, emotional, and mental well-being is vital for creating resilience. This may involve getting adequate sleep, eating healthily, exercising frequently, and engaging in things that offer us joy and relaxation.

Seeking assistance: Building a support network of friends, family members, and trusted professionals can offer us the encouragement, direction, and perspective we need to handle challenging situations with resilience.

Setting objectives and taking action: Setting realistic goals and making tiny efforts towards achieving them might help us reclaim a sense of control and agency in the face of hardship.

Practicing thankfulness: Cultivating a practice of gratitude can help us change our emphasis from what is lacking to what we have, fostering a sense of resilience and optimism in the face of hardships.

Chapter 6

Finding Opportunity in Challenge

Life is full of problems, obstacles, and disappointments that can leave us feeling overwhelmed, discouraged, and uncertain of the future. Yet, within the center of every obstacle lies the possibility for development, resilience, and transformation. In this chapter, we will explore the topic of finding opportunity in hardship, revealing the hidden treasures and lessons that adversity has to offer. Drawing upon concepts from psychology, neurology, and personal development, we will study how reframing challenges as opportunities can empower us to accept change, overcome hurdles, and thrive in the face of adversity.

i. Embracing a Growth Mindset

At the foundation of discovering opportunity in struggle lies the mindset with which we tackle challenging situations. In this section, we will study the concept of a growth mindset, which entails viewing problems as opportunities for learning and growth rather than as threats to our sense of self-worth or competence. By embracing a growth mindset, we may reframe adversity as a catalyst for personal and professional development, empowering us to face problems with curiosity, resilience, and optimism.

ii. Cultivating Resilience

Resilience is the ability to bounce back from adversity, adapt to change, and prosper in the face of adversity. In this section, we will explore ways to foster resilience in our daily lives, including practicing self-care, seeking support, and reframing negative beliefs. By fostering our resilience, we may face adversities with grace, courage, and resilience, emerging stronger and more resilient on the other side.

iii. Finding Meaning and Purpose

One of the main qualities that enable individuals to find opportunity in difficulty is the ability to find meaning and purpose in tough events. In this section, we will explore ways to build a sense of meaning and purpose during adversity, including meditation, introspection, and engaging in activities that connect with our values and passions. By discovering meaning and purpose in adversity, we may transform even the most painful events into opportunities for growth, connection, and fulfillment.

iv. Fostering adaptability and flexibility

In a world marked by rapid change and unpredictability, adaptation and flexibility are crucial talents for discovering opportunities in difficulty. In this section, we will explore ways to build adaptation and flexibility in our lives, including embracing ambiguity, reframing setbacks as chances for growth, and cultivating a mindset of inquiry and exploration. By embracing change with openness and flexibility, we may negotiate problems with resilience and creativity, grabbing the opportunities that come with difficulty.

v. Accepting Failure as a Stepping Stone to Success

Failure is an unavoidable component of the path that leads to individual development and accomplishment. In this section, we will explore the concept of embracing failure as a stepping stone to success and reframing setbacks as chances for learning and progress. By viewing failure not as a reflection of our worth or ability but as a natural and necessary component of the learning process, we can tackle difficulties with increased resilience, courage, and commitment.

vi. Cultivating Gratitude and Optimism

Gratitude and optimism are excellent antidotes to the negativity and despair that often follow struggle. In this section, we will explore ways to foster thankfulness and optimism in our daily lives, including maintaining a gratitude diary, practicing mindfulness, and reframing negative ideas. By establishing an attitude of thankfulness and optimism, we may shift our emphasis from what is lacking to what we have, fostering a sense of resilience, hope, and well-being in the face of hardship.

vii. Seeking Opportunities for Growth and Learning

Even in the middle of difficulties, there are possibilities for growth, learning, and self-discovery. In this section, we will discuss ways of identifying opportunities for growth and learning during the struggle, including venturing outside of our comfort zones, embracing ambiguity, and requesting feedback and constructive criticism. By embracing problems with curiosity and a willingness to learn, we can uncover the hidden treasures and opportunities that adversity has to offer, propelling us toward personal and professional progress and fulfillment.

Chapter 7

Cultivating a Growth Mindset: Embracing the Power of Growth and Learning

In life, we are presented with a plethora of problems, setbacks, and barriers that can either hamper our progress or propel us toward growth and achievement. At the heart of our capacity to negotiate these problems lies our mindset—the beliefs and attitudes that define how we perceive ourselves, our skills, and the world around us. In this chapter, we will explore the concept of creating a growth mindset, a belief system that embraces the power of growth, resilience, and learning in the face of adversity. Drawing upon insights from psychology, neuroscience, and personal development, we will reveal the key principles and practices that enable individuals to create a growth mindset and unlock their full potential.

i. Understanding the Growth Mindset

The concept of a growth mindset was developed by psychologist Carol Dweck, who found that individuals who believe that their abilities can be developed through dedication and hard work—a growth mindset—are more likely to achieve success and fulfillment compared to those who believe that their abilities are fixed and immutable—a fixed mindset. In a growth mindset, problems are regarded as chances for progress, failures are considered learning experiences, and effort is seen as the way to mastery.

ii. Embracing Challenges as Opportunities for Growth

In a growth mindset, problems are not perceived as threats to our sense of self-worth or competence but rather as chances for growth and learning. Instead of avoiding problems or giving up when faced with hardship, individuals with a growth mindset welcome challenges with curiosity and perseverance, viewing them as chances to extend themselves, gain new skills, and increase their capacities.

iii. Viewing Failure as a Stepping Stone to Success

There will always be times when you fail on your road to success. In a growth mindset, failure is not considered a reflection of our worth or ability but rather a natural and necessary component of the learning process. Instead of being discouraged by failure, people with a growth mindset see it as a chance to learn, grow, and get better. They accept failure as a stepping stone to success, regarding setbacks as temporary and surmountable barriers on the way to mastery.

Chapter 8

Conflict Transformation: Moving Beyond Resolution

Conflict is a natural and inevitable element of human contact, coming from differences in values, views, and viewpoints. While traditional approaches to conflict resolution focus on finding a settlement or compromise, conflict transformation tries to address the underlying causes of conflict and provide chances for positive change and progress. In this chapter, we will explore the notion of conflict transformation, exposing its principles, methods, and possibilities for achieving enduring change in individuals, relationships, and communities. Drawing upon principles from conflict resolution theory, peace studies, and social psychology, we will study how conflict transformation enables us to proceed beyond resolution toward reconciliation, healing, and empowerment.

i. Understanding Conflict Transformation

Conflict transformation is a holistic approach to conflict that tries to address the core causes of conflict and offer possibilities for positive change and progress. Unlike traditional approaches to conflict resolution, which focus on obtaining a settlement or compromise, conflict transformation tries to modify the fundamental dynamics of conflict, developing understanding, empathy, and collaboration among those involved. In this section, we will study the concepts of conflict transformation, including the significance of addressing power imbalances, creating connections, and facilitating discussion and reconciliation.

ii. Moving Beyond Win-Lose Dynamics

Traditional techniques for dispute resolution often perpetuate win-lose dynamics, where one party emerges as the winner and the other as the loser. In contrast, conflict transformation strives to go beyond win-lose dynamics towards win-win solutions that benefit all parties involved. In this section, we will explore tactics for establishing win-win solutions to conflict, including interest-based negotiating, consensus-building, and collaborative problem-solving. By developing mutual understanding and cooperation, conflict transformation helps parties move beyond combative viewpoints toward mutually beneficial results.

iii. Fostering Empathy and Understanding

Empathy is a strong tool for altering conflict, enabling parties to see beyond their views and comprehend the feelings and needs of others. In this section, we will study tactics for promoting empathy and understanding in the middle of conflict, including active listening, perspective-taking, and empathic communication. By building empathy, parties can build bridges of understanding and connection, providing the road for reconciliation and healing.

iv. Addressing structural injustice and inequality

Conflict is typically rooted in systemic issues of injustice, inequality, and oppression. In this section, we will study the role of conflict transformation in addressing structural causes of conflict, such as prejudice, poverty, and social marginalization. By working to address these core causes, conflict transformation attempts to create more just and equitable societies where all individuals have the opportunity to thrive and contribute to the common good.

v. Promoting Healing and Reconciliation

Healing and reconciliation are important aims of conflict transformation, helping parties to move beyond past grievances and build a more positive and constructive future together. In this section, we will study ways to encourage healing and reconciliation in the aftermath of conflict, including truth-telling, apology, forgiveness, and restorative justice processes. By giving parties opportunities to address past damages, express remorse, and seek forgiveness, conflict transformation encourages healing and reconciliation at both individual and community levels.

vi. Empowering Individuals and Communities

Conflict transformation is ultimately about encouraging individuals and communities to take control of their conflicts and work towards positive change and growth. In this section, we will study options for empowering individuals and communities to become active agents of conflict transformation, including education, training, and capacity-building programs. By equipping individuals with the knowledge, skills, and resources they need to manage conflict constructively, conflict transformation enables them to become catalysts for good change in their own lives and communities.

Chapter 9

Turning Setbacks into Stepping Stones: Harnessing Adversity for Growth and Success.

Setbacks are an inherent part of life's journey, requiring us to confront adversity, overcome barriers, and persevere in the pursuit of our objectives and dreams. While losses can be depressing and disheartening, they also present us with possibilities for growth, learning, and self-discovery. In this chapter, we will explore the concept of turning setbacks into stepping stones, unearthing the perseverance, power, and insight that may arise from hardship. Drawing upon principles from psychology, personal development, and philosophy, we will study ways to utilize setbacks as catalysts for growth, change, and eventually success.

i. Understanding Setbacks

Setbacks come in various forms, from personal failings and disappointments to unexpected hurdles and obstacles. In this section, we will study the nature of setbacks, analyzing their many causes, repercussions, and implications for our lives and ambitions. By understanding the nature of setbacks, we can acquire the resilience and perseverance needed to manage adversity and emerge stronger and more resilient on the other side.

ii. Accepting failure as a prelude to achievement

Failure is a natural and inevitable part of the journey towards growth and achievement. In this section, we will explore the concept of embracing failure as a prelude to achievement and reframing setbacks as chances for learning, growth, and self-improvement. By viewing failure not as a reflection of our worth or ability but as a necessary and valuable component of the learning process, we may tackle setbacks with courage, resilience, and persistence.

iii. Cultivating Resilience in the Face of Adversity.

Resilience is the ability to bounce back from adversity, adapt to change, and prosper in the face of adversity. In this section, we will discuss ways to foster resilience in the face of setbacks, including practicing self-care, seeking help, and reframing negative beliefs. By fostering our resilience, we may endure setbacks with grace, courage, and resilience, emerging stronger and more resilient on the other side.

iv. Finding Meaning and Purpose in Adversity

Adversity can develop our character, deepen our values, and clarify our sense of purpose and direction in life. In this section, we will explore ways to find meaning and purpose in adversity, including reflection, introspection, and engaging in activities that connect with our values and passions. By discovering meaning and purpose in adversity, we can transform setbacks into opportunities for growth, self-discovery, and personal fulfillment.

v. Turning Obstacles into Opportunities

Obstacles are often hidden possibilities for growth and transformation. In this section, we will discuss ways to turn obstacles into opportunities, including reframing issues as possibilities for learning, creativity, and innovation. By confronting challenges with curiosity, flexibility, and a willingness to learn, we can harness their transforming power to propel us toward our goals and aspirations.

vi. Cultivating a Growth Mindset

At the heart of converting setbacks into stepping stones lies the mindset with which we face obstacles. In this section, we will study the concept of a growth mindset, which involves perceiving setbacks as chances for growth, learning, and self-improvement. By embracing a growth mindset, we may reframe setbacks as transitory setbacks on the route to success, empowering us to persevere in the face of adversity and ultimately achieve our goals and aspirations.

vii. Seeking support and guidance

Navigating setbacks can be tough and overwhelming, but we do not have to do it alone. In this section, we will explore the value of obtaining help and direction from others, including friends, family members, mentors, and trusted experts. By surrounding ourselves with helpful and loving others, we can get perspective, encouragement, and guidance to help us handle adversities with courage, resilience, and resolve.

Conclusion

Sailing into the Future: Charting Your Course of Thrive

In the voyage of life, we are individually captains of our ships, navigating the vast and often unpredictable seas of existence. Along the way, we meet storms, turbulent waters, and unforeseen difficulties that test our resolve, our perseverance, and our dedication to our chosen course. Yet, despite the turbulence and unpredictability, there lies the potential to chart a path to thrive—to guide our ships toward a destination of fulfillment, progress, and purpose. As we reflect on the lessons gained and construct our resilience plans, we set sail into the future with courage, drive, and a persistent commitment to thrive in the face of adversity.

i. Reflecting on Lessons Learned

Reflection is the compass that directs us on our journey, enabling us to gain insight, wisdom, and clarity from our experiences—both victories and sorrows. As we reflect on the lessons learned from our past, we unearth vital insights about ourselves, our abilities, and our opportunities for improvement. We see the patterns and themes that have molded our path thus far, and we take insight from the struggles we have overcome and the setbacks we have faced. In reflecting on our lessons learned, we develop a greater insight into who we are and where we want to go, empowering us to chart a course to thrive with purpose and intention.

ii. Creating Your Personal Resilience Plan

Resilience is the anchor that keeps us stable in the face of misfortune, helping us to withstand the storms of life with grace, courage, and resolve. As we construct our personal resilience plans, we draw upon the lessons learned from our prior experiences and the insights received from our reflections. We discover the strengths, resources, and support systems that will buttress us in times of challenge, and we establish strategies for fostering our resilience and well-being daily. Our resilience plan is our roadmap for navigating the ups and downs of life, giving us the tools and resources we need to thrive in the face of hardship and uncertainty.

Finally,As we set sail into the future, setting our route to thrive, we do it with a sense of purpose, resilience, and hope. We carry with us the lessons learned from our past experiences, drawing upon their wisdom and insight to assist us on our journey forward. We welcome the challenges and opportunities that lie ahead, knowing that each obstacle we experience is an opportunity for growth, learning, and self-discovery. We develop our personal resilience plans, providing ourselves with the tools, resources, and support networks we need to sail the unexpected waters of life with courage, grace, and resilience.

In mapping our course to thrive, we realize that the journey is not always plain sailing—there will be storms, rough waves, and unforeseen challenges along the way. But it is in managing these hurdles that we discover our true strength, resilience, and ability for growth. And it is in embracing the voyage—with all its twists and turns, victories and hardships—that we truly come alive, sailing into the future with a sense of purpose, passion, and possibilities.

So let us set sail into the future, charting our course to thrive with courage, dedication, and a solid resolve to embrace the adventure, whatever it may bring. For in the journey of life, it is not the destination that matters.

www.ingramcontent.com/pod-product-compliance
Lightning Source LLC
Chambersburg PA
CBHW070347230526
45471CB00006B/2450